Cornebo's Santa's Sleigh Jokes

Author
Brian Daniel Starr

Cornebo's Santa's Sleigh Jokes

ISBN-13: 978-0-359-93636-6

LCCN: 2019914917

Published with an Act of Congress

Printed in the United States of America

Dedicated to my Authorship and
Pen Pals
Who have given me the
Patience and fortitude to
Complete this work

Also to the People in WW2 who
put their faith in the Star

Table of Contents

Section X Wife Jokes

NOTE THIS JOKE IS BAD IT DID NOT GET IN THE TABLE OF CONTENTS

Yes Short Whits are deaf, but hopefully they will grow up and have ears, until then the Priest is stuck on Braille, They cant even hear the horseplay in the workplace to know when their Joke is recited. .... (just one more dollar please for the Best Friend of the Library !!!) No Hell No. Its for the Constitution in Braille !!! No Hel No. Aw Mummy Just Kidding !!! Go away Amon – Ra, Dad is busy making Law !!! No He No !!!

The corns about a foot high and nude like the Geico Lizard !!!

One Liners

Castrate human castilligioan (like Isabella) Oh Eliza Please
Trumball Trumpetter Dictatorship x wife jokes see the nip fools

Hello Mr. Marine at the Marinnara

use of opiate as afrodesiact as found in Vulgate page 777 and 616 by Tiitle holder Daniel Marine

This is Joke for a Header with no Widows or Orphans

Hi Weekly !!

There is no such thing as a Menestrating Dom. Bitching Horse Nuri

Its Not Over Yet (4 years on Grandpa's Birthday) Yeah

shaw salem sahibe knight from islam holy herine war
Fornification under command of King Danielco

Emanciation not allowed.

get your own way to enslave Mr. President horsey

Electric Arcs do better than Lethal Injection !!!

electronic manipulation without prosecution is illegal as well as done by Obama administration and office of homeland security resulting in torture and *their very* by their new top head of department Kevin

Poor thing is Not a Torey regardless of the Spelling !!

LOndon keyes for President the female oriental majority

Poor thing is Not a Torey regardless of the Spelling !!

Moral of the Story is Live in a county with at least one military base and do not Share.

addicts on horse local dandelion wine dont beat horse I am not just on Vodka either letters H for horse w for whiskey the horse

This is Joke for a Header with no Widows or Orphans

And Let the Trustees Recgonize Gravity !!!

Durham Guys Signs !

This neighborhood has People carry weapons on Drugs !!

Intelligent Star Gazers on the Ocean !!!

Like Sib Says He aint heavy hes my brother and hes not Blood line. !! (uncles Beware the Stalks are Deaf !!

Jokes from the Evil Grave Yard Watcher Farm Guy

Don Starr (not my Godfather)

Stay away from that one Genealogist !!!

This is not Syndicated Commercials

Old Mac Don's Farm

From 5 Families in Chicagoland and New York !!

Whats our Address ?

No Horse Head for U !!

Ruths Stone

I was Lik -ed

This is Joke for a Header with no Widows or Orphans

but but it was my first Master Grandson
I gave the Horse shoe at 8 years old

and Oh Yeah Dorothea -- The tailesmen of Leo anti anything like this Brass B

This is Joke for a Header with no Widows or Orphans

I hear Great Grannie Faye Starr Speaks Honorary Lakota !!!

(from New France) the 700 club year of Anniversary of the Blessing of Charlemagne Brass is still on the Key Ring)

This is Joke for a Header with no Widows or Orphans

(From Sweden I keep the Key of Olaf !!! with Rumors

(From Electronic FOB guy my) I did not go in today ! I was out to lunch

From Table Grave Lefty, Sam Starr Hey U Gholulash . save some for me.

(DAmn Worms) !!!

Automotive?

The Medal A rust is in the field; while the falcon from Plymouth (Plymath) Falcon is sold.

Speaking Afterlife (Book Plug)

Gramps?

Yes Major Squire Brian ?

If u lik Grandma Ruth why she need help from Home Wrecker (swats the Fly!) when she is dead at at such a young age?

I Don't know (Smash ram Nose Bert) YOu mean my sib?

Ruth ? Starr?

Upon Advisement from Dad no personal information attainable until Federal Census Release every 72 years, (Great Grandpa Elwin had a Guersey, its on the Federal Census) Dan has got to eat !!!

So u don’t use names just the word Living (no Rabbit tongue for u Daughter of Tyre !!)

Living Great Ant Starr? or Living Mom and Pop Starr?

at 1938 ----->

For u Master squire Ruth

Lamna Quadrilla Derfilla and Firfita

For u Master Corpse

Ruth Quadrilla Derfilla Firfita (and Brothers of Master Corpse.

This is Joke for a Header with no Widows or Orphans

DRAW !!!

29 palms?

REport as charged, shoot the dirt !!!

Agent 99- Army Square ASh for El main to dah from 1920--- Glen Campbel's Mom is still Older and Slower.

This is Joke for a Header with no Widows or Orphans

To Every E1 No Name in the Army

Course you know we's all Christians, and your best bet at E2 is EWE, and the W aint allowed if you a Beetle, you gonna enjoy !!!

U r Me!   And u and I.

Ohio Roadway

Motorists are on Drugs (if the event of porshe attack or impact from either young Homeland Security or Mafia or Knights) use a good trump, On the pedal with electric Boost.

Automotiveation Nation !!!

My 2000 + 5 Honda with Electria Boost worked in the Lone Star State (Hey loan Shark whats the Badge.)

This is Joke for a Header with no Widows or Orphans

You Aint Osage u Lone Star !!! Oits still law !!!

Hey U Cheyenne shot El Dorado and ATE !!! Wheres the skinned Pelt !!! Do I need o send ARmy Sarege Ast to Starr County ?

Tommy Gun ain't Peter Gun. !

Gum Shoes are Stupid.   Fetters on the Mirrors.

The Following is a reprint of Cornebo's Dirty Jokes

with Cleanser, Figuring the cost of a page is not much to print such Cyphers of Lou, (like the Azazalia song of the Frying Plant agent Pine) (Don't Pine for Me with your dirty joke !!!)

This is Joke for a Header with no Widows or Orphans

NOTE:

An honorable discharge from the Ship People means Star Board is on the Right   Always, and Yes Portales I will have a lemonade !!!

PIG

Pig fell in the mud.

Camel

Private was in the service in the desert. He asked the sarge, what about the women? Sarge said the camel's out back.

So private went out to look at the camel and lifted up the tail and looked at it and said no not today.

A few weeks later the Private goes out and lifts the table and proceeds to satisfy himself with the camel. The camel starts making horrible sounds.

The Sarge leans out the window and screams out to the private,

No No ride the camel to town where the girls are!!!!!

Lovers in the Shower

Two guys are in the shower and one says just a minute I have got to go don't do anything until I come back.

The guy says ok.

A few minutes later the guy comes back and sees a wad of sperm on the wall.

He says I thought I told you to wait.

The guy says I did, I farted.

Dead Mermaid and the Cow

A family of a mom and dad and three strong boys are living near the river. They had a cow and everyday they used the cow for their food.

One day the youngest boy woke up and found the cow was dead.

So he decided to go throw himself in the river. On the way he finds a mermaid. The mermaid asks what he is doing. He explains about the cow and the mermaid says, you look pretty strong, if you can make love to me five times I will restore the cow to life. So he says ok and they start loving and he does it until 4 times and gives up. So the mermaid allows him to throw himself in the river.

So the next boy wakes up and sees the dead cow, and decides to go throw himself in the river. He notices his little brother is missing. So on the way he meets the mermaid. The mermaid tells him about his brother and offers that if he can make love to the mermaid ten times she will restore the dead cow and his brother to life. So he agrees and they start loving and after eight times he says he cannot anymore, so the mermaid allows himself to throw himself into the river.

So the strongest oldest boy wakes up and sees the dead cow and decides to go down to the river. He finds the mermaid and says hey baby whats up. The mermaid explains about the two brothers and offers to make love to the young man and if he can go 15 times she offers to restore the two brothers and the cow.

The strong young man says ok that sounds ok about me brothers and the cow, but how do I know you won't drop dead after ten times like the cow did !!!!!

Mountain Goat

Dedicated to Cornebo's Dad the older Cornebo

Did you know mountain goats are designed for mountains. Sure, one leg is shorter on the right then the left so they can go around the mountain and not have a problem. Only thing is if they turn around then they fall down !!!! I believe it.

Rabbi and Priest Sex and Ham

The Priest asks the Rabbi, have you ever violated the dietary requirements about eating pork.

The rabbi says yes father, I once ate some ham.

Then the rabbi asks the father, he says you are a celibate priest, have to ever loved a women in a carnal way.

The father yes Rabbi I really must confess, once I did.

The Rabbi says you got to admit it beats the hell out of Ham!!!!!!!

Four Preachers and the Priest.

An Episcopal, a Prespaterian, and a Methodist and a Baptist preacher are all seen going to the red house where the ladies work hard all night. The police staking out the joint are really upset because they decided to let each one go because they were clergy. They were really worried they might not get a collar and get a chance to visit with the girls. Then they saw the local priest go in.

The cops both said, Oh no, I wonder which one of the girls died!!!!!

Fluffy the Bunny

A man lived next to an old widow. She had a pet bunny she named fluffy. No other family. The man had a large mastic dog. One day the man came home and the dog had fluffy in his mouth, Fluffy was dead, bloody and dirty. So the man decided he would try to cover for the dog, so he got Fluffy inside, cleaned him, hair dryed his hair and put him back in his cage.

A week later the man was leaving his house when he met the old widow. She said hello and asked if he heard about the death in her family. She said Fluffy had died. Then she said the funny thing was someone dug her up, cleaned her off, and put her back in her cage !!!!!!

Fat Ass General Johnson

A man worked at the motor pool with a squad of other enlisted.

One day a call came thru and the caller said if there were any vehicles in the motor pool

The Prive said nothing but General Fat Ass Johnson's jeep.

The caller said do you know who this is!!!! I am General Johnson!!!

The Prive said do you know who this is? The General said no in outrage.

The prive said good and hung up. Click………….

Hurricane Bessie

There was a girl that worked the red house and had a routine. She asked her client if he would let her be Hurricane Bessie.

The client said sure. So she pissed all over him and said I am hurricane Bessie and that is the warm hurricane water that is swirling all around you.

He said God Damn

She then took her giant boobs and proceeded to beat his head with both of them and said This is hurricane Bessie and these are the large coconuts that are falling from the trees.

He said God Damn it I am leaving.

Hurricane Bessie said Why are you leaving.

He said Who can fuck in this kind of weather. !!!!

A man was out fishing

There was a man who was fishing and had put his fish in the bucket.

The game warden came up and said let me see your fishing license.

The man said what for these are my pet fish. I keep them in my bathtub and I let them out here at the lake, they swim and get some exercise and come back and I take them home.

The Game warden says I don't believe you let me see.

So the man takes the bucket and sets all the fish into the lake for their exercise.

The game warden comes back and says when are the fish coming back.

The man says What Fish ?????

Aamish Date.

A young man and his fiancée are out in the winter in their horse and buggy and the man says to his girl my popsicle is really cold, could you please put your hand around it and keep it warm. He indicates his dick. She says sure and proceeds to warm it up. He sighs and she says look it melted !!!!!!

Saint Peter and Heaven with Bill

A man comes up to heaven and says I hear Bill Clinton is here.

Saint Peter says yes he checked in a few months ago, you can go meet him;

The man says he would really like to meet the virgin,

Saint peter hangs his head in shame and says, well we call her mary now, you see Bill checked in a few months ago………

Saint Peter and the defender.

Saint Peter says what brings you hear.

The man says he was stopping a rape of a motorcycle gang and a women and somehow he ended up here................

A Group of Blonds

There was a group of five blonds, all pretty.

They come in to the bar with a puzzle of Elmo all glued and fastened on a board and shellaced.

The bar tender says why is this such a celebration?

The blonds say look how good we are. It took the five of us only three weeks to get this puzzle done and look on the box, it says three years and up…………

A Man on the Elevator and the Blond walks in

The blond says tgif. The man says shit.

The blond says tgif. The man says shit.

The blond angry now says thank god its Friday.

The man says Sorry Honey its Thursday.

Blond curtains on the computer. Curtains for u.

A man asks the blond why did she put curtains on her computer screen.

She says that she heard it was windows.

Road Breakdown

An Electical engineer a chemical engineer and a Microsoft engineer are traveling on business and the car shuts down.

The driver pulls over and says I am the Electrical engineer I will check the electrical system and see if we can go.

The chemical engineer says good idea I can check the fuel system and see if we can go.

The Microsoft engineer says no problem just roll down the windows and roll them up again and go.

Mr. and Mrs. Foote

Mr. and Mrs. Foot lived in foot ville. They had a little foot.

One day the child foot got ill so Mr. and Mrs. Foot took the child to the foot doctor. The foot doctor told Mr. and Mrs Foote the child was going to die. Mr. and Mrs. Foote prayed constantly but it did not work and one day the child foot kicked the bucket.

So Mr. and Mrs. Foote buried their child and mourned for may years. One day Mrs. Foote got sick so Mr. Foote took Mrs. Foote to the Foote doctor. The foote doctor told Mr. Foote that Mrs. Foote was going to die. Mr. Foote frowned and said that cannot be I already have one foote in the grave.

This is Joke for a Header with no Widows or Orphans

www.ingramcontent.com/pod-product-compliance
Ingram Content Group UK Ltd.
Pitfield, Milton Keynes, MK11 3LW, UK
UKHW041839200726
13854UKWH00003BA/1224